ABOUT
REVELS

• A Collection of Essays •
Directors' Notes, Historical Commentary
and Personal Reflections

Compiled & Edited by
ELIZABETH LLOYD MAYER

One-Stroke Brushwork Circles by
KAZUAKI TANAHASHI

ISBN 0-9705065-0-3

CALIFORNIA REVELS
337 17th Street, Suite 207
Oakland, California, 94612
Phone: (510) 452-9334
Fax: (510) 452-9335
www.calrevels.org

Table of Contents

Dedication

FOR ANDREW T. WILLIAMS, in grateful recognition of his remarkable leadership, steadfast vision, and devoted service to California Revels.

• Acknowledgements

California Revels thanks Karoline De Martini, Kathy Fitzgerald, Linda Hess, Jenny Kee, Sue Jennison, Kathryn Pritchett, Gail Richard, Dennis Roland, Andrew and Linda Williams, and most especially Kelci Cell, for devoted and expert assistance in compiling this collection. We thank Mary Gene Myer and the Washington D.C. Revels for their "Revels Readings," Revels, Inc. for material previously printed in programs of Cambridge Revels productions, and the authors of those pieces for generous permission to excerpt, revise and edit them into essays for this collection. We are especially grateful to Gayle Rich, Patrick Swanson, Alan Casso and Sue Ladr of Revels, Inc. for their support. We acknowledge Kazimierz Godz for the original concept of the multiple Zen circle used in this book. Finally, we thank John Langstaff, whose indefatigable involvement in every phase of this project has once again proven him — in Susan Cooper's felicitous phrase — the onlie begetter of the Revels.

Publication of this book was made possible by an anonymous gift "in honor of the community Revels creates," and by the Virginia Wellington Cabot Foundation, Kathy Cabot Fitzgerald, Janie and Jeffrey Green, the Ithaka Foundation, Nion and Ira McEvoy, and finally, Mrs. Charles F. Lowrey, godmother and valued advisor to California Revels since its inception.

Preface

P E O P L E need celebration. We need those wild and holy expressions of who we are which lift us out of isolation and into connection with each other. We need moments which inject the ordinary with awe and engage our capacities for the extraordinary. Celebration does that. And Revels does that.

The distinctive thing about Revels as a form of theater is the way it pairs ritual with performance. When I first imagined this collection of essays, that juxtaposition struck me as key — key to the way Revels takes theater and turns it into a vehicle for celebration. In sorting through the many pieces written about Revels over the years, I found wonderful descriptions of how that juxtaposition works and how it infuses Revels with celebration.

But evocative as all those pieces were, I kept feeling that a book about Revels wanted more than words, more than an appeal to our all-too-verbal sensibilities. At that point I happened to meet Kazuaki Tanahashi, among the world's leading one-stroke brushwork artists and originator of its contemporary form. I visited his studio with Revels founder John Langstaff, and Kaz showed us his work. We were especially drawn to a series of circular brushwork images.

The Zen circle, Kaz explained, represents enlightenment: the experience of completeness in each moment. Always the same completeness, never the same moment. So with the one-stroke circle — always the same form but unique every time it is drawn with a brush. It seemed a vivid image for the peculiar fusion of ritual and performance which Revels concocts as theater. The power of ritual lies in accumulated repetition, the perpetual sameness of essential form. The power of performance lies in the unrepeatable moment – the fact that performance happens always for the first and only time.

Revels puts that conjunction on stage, giving vital theatrical shape to the way life's continuity contains change, familiarity holds surprise. The essence of Revels lives in celebrating the paradox, in celebrating the place where light and darkness, awe and irreverence, need and abundance, grief and exultation, living and dying, encounter each other and merge.

• Elizabeth Lloyd Mayer
20 September 2000

• Postscript

Just before this book went to press, Kaz and I spoke again.

"I've been thinking," he said. "I want to show you something."

I went to his studio and he produced a folder of several circles – not, this time, the single circles I'd seen before. Instead, they were multiple circles, one layered on top of another but still the product of only one brush stroke.

"Perhaps these are better for Revels," said Kaz. "Revels is built out of multiplicity – multiple forms of music, dance, poetry, drama, ritual. Besides, these are the first multiple circles I've done. Since I began showing the single circle twenty years ago, it's been used a lot. Perhaps Revels would like to be the first to show this new form."

Of course I accepted – with delight. Hence, the multiple circles. A single circle still illuminates the title page of each essay.

The Beginnings of Revels

John Langstaff

THE REVELS may well have started with our family carol parties. My mother and father began inviting friends to sing carols on the Sunday night before Christmas in 1920, the year I was born. I soon joined their musical party: hearing my father sing the ballad of "King Herod and the Cock" with my mother at the piano, miming the Page to his King Wenceslas, struggling to remember to sing out at the right moment when verses of the "The Twelve Days of Christmas" were divided among the family, and singing "The Friendly Beasts" with my brothers and sister. The guests, crowded into the candlelit house in Brooklyn Heights, joined in singing the well-known carols and our favorite Bach chorales and rounds. The spicy smell of hot wassail brewing on the stove all day permeated the house.

The caroling "waits" met on Christmas Eve, my birthday, at our house. My parents would lead the singers out into the streets and from house to house through the Heights, gathering more and more neighbors to sing as the night progressed. Later, as a choirboy at Grace Church in New York, I took part in the candlelight processionals, singing the magnificent Christmas music of the carol services.

At the heart of all the music and all the celebration was the Winter Solstice – that cold, dark time when the year turns again towards the coming of light. The Solstice has been honored by people since ancient times and has always been at the core of our December Revels performances. We once lived our lives in close touch with the changing seasons, always wondering what might or might not come to pass at the darkest time of year, hoping that our song, our mime, and our dance could work as a propitiation to Nature, ensuring the return of Spring, of warmth and of new life. Many of our winter carols reflect these ancient hopes and fears.

My love of the carols and traditional music I grew up with eventually broadened into a fascination with folk material of every sort – rituals, music, dancing and drama. All have become essential elements in Revels. Revels' focus on active audience involvement grew out of those same roots, and especially out of my awareness that few things bond people as powerfully as singing together.

In my career as a concert singer, I often longed to step off the stage and bring that kind of involvement to my audience. So, in the very first Revels performance at New York City's Town Hall in 1956, I drew on many of those elements, starting with my own earliest experiences: my family's music parties, the pageantry of Grace Church and my father's extensive carol collection, as well as the folk music I had continued to learn from traditional singers and dancers throughout my life.

From there Revels has developed in ways I never could have anticipated and certainly couldn't have planned. New cities form new companies, new scripts are written, new directors come on board, and exciting new performers from a vast array of cultures keep joining us.

And that, after all, is the way it should be. That's how folk-tradition grows: organically, unpredictably, drawing people together in powerful celebration of their shared humanity.

Reflections on Defining Revels

Elizabeth Lloyd Mayer

A STAFF MEMBER from the National Endowment for the Arts once commented that he found it impossible to place Revels within conventional performing arts categories. Revels, he said, isn't a concert, nor is it a play. It doesn't fall within our usual definition of music theater, since it's neither opera nor Broadway musical. Instead, he suggested, Revels really constitutes a distinct performance genre, a new form of music theater.

As of December 2000, Revels productions are now established in eleven cities (Cambridge, MA; Chicago, IL; Hanover, NH; Houston, TX; Minneapolis, MN; New York, NY; Philadelphia, PA; Portland, OR; Tacoma, WA; Washington, DC; and the San Francisco Bay Area). Each year, productions play to over 80,000 audience members. Requests to be the next city hosting a Revels production arrive regularly and from all over the country. They arrive at a rate that far exceeds Revels' capacity to reproduce itself. Each request is characterized by a fascinating determination to possess a local version of this thing called Revels.

What is the appeal? Why, in cities with thriving and widely varied offerings in the performing arts, are people determined to add Revels to what they've already got?

Answering that question means, I think, spelling out what Revels is, as well as what it offers that may be distinctive. A good place to start might be with the NEA staffer and his suggestion that Revels constitutes an actual theatrical form,

different in kind from those with which we're convention-
ally familiar.

It's a provocative suggestion. I believe we may get furthest
with developing it if we move outside traditional theater ter-
minology and consider the idea of liturgy. Because of its asso-
ciation with religion, the notion of liturgy as a form of theater
– as a form, particularly, of secular theater – is unfamiliar. Yet
if we ignore connotation and go back to roots, liturgy has
nothing to do with religion. Liturgy means literally "work of
the people" (from "*leit*," people; and "*ergos*," work).

Loosely speaking, there's something tantalizing about the
idea of Revels as "work of the people." Every Revels performance contains those crucial moments which mobilize
an entire audience to joined action. Explicitly, the action is
scripted as song or as dance. But under the surface, whatever
form the action takes, the joining and the action have a distinct function. They aim to ignite a collective human purpose: they aim at sparking shared awareness of the perpetual
human endeavor to bring light out of darkness and hope out
of despair. That, if anything, is the essence of Revels.

It's what Susan Cooper speaks of in *The Shortest Day*, a poem
that has become a ritual component of every Revels that
builds its theme around the Winter Solstice.

> *...And everywhere, down the centuries of the snow-white world,*
> *Came people, singing, dancing,*
> *To drive the dark away.*
> *They lighted candles in the winter trees;*
> *They hung their homes with evergreen,*
> *They burned beseeching fires all night long*
> *To keep the year alive....*

People work to drive the dark away and **people** work to keep the year alive. People play a part in bringing back hope, in bringing back the light. Perhaps we can call that "work of the people."

But now back to the question of liturgy as a specific theatrical form. Liturgy is distinguished from traditional drama in the looseness of structure within which elements are strung together. Liturgy combines music, movement, story, song and poetry to comprise a highly crafted whole that lacks a specific story line. The art of liturgy consists in the art of mingling its component elements: building them to evoke mood and meaning. Over centuries, the great religious liturgies have developed this art. Much of our finest music and poetry are by-products; they were once intrinsic pieces of what made liturgy work. The structure of liturgy depended on those pieces to function as moments of great beauty, deliberately transformational, intended to lift people out of daily life into an experience beyond themselves and beyond their own capacities. Meantime, those same liturgies also relied on the ordinary. Elements that served to invite and to welcome were as important as elements that served to inspire. The art of constructing liturgy lies in constructing precisely that paradox: the integration of ordinary with extraordinary, participation with awe.

The art of constructing Revels lies close to that same paradox. To the extent that such a paradox defines the effectiveness of liturgy, it may help define what's essential in the structure of Revels. It may help explain why people who don't like sing-alongs find that they feel like singing when they come to Revels. It may also help draw the contrast between traditional theater and Revels. Traditional theater depends on plots. But a story line that's too tightly delineated may defeat exactly what makes Revels work. Plots, by their nature, define who's on stage and who isn't. Plots dictate that, no matter how engaged, the audience remains outside the story. In Revels, as in liturgy, the boundaries are more fluid. Performance on the stage moves deliberately off the stage, into participation with the audience. But equally important, on-stage performance extricates itself from off-stage participation. There must be moments in which performers exceed what an audience can do, in which those on-stage create something brilliantly transporting for those off-stage.

Revels is not about religion. But insofar as the dramatic form we employ draws on what I've called liturgical, it may be that we show our debt to an art form that has belonged primarily to religion. Perhaps, in claiming the structure of liturgy for Revels, we aim at claiming liturgy as a specific and secular dramatic form: a generic *"work of the people."*

A Dream of Revels

Susan Cooper

ANY CHRISTMAS TIME at Harvard University's Sanders Theater in Cambridge, Massachusetts. The snow is deep outside. Into the cavernous, echoing lobby stream hundreds of families, all the generations mixed, coat-wrapped and scarf-wound, their breath clouding in the cold air. Christmas is in their heads and this is a peak of it: their anticipated celebration, familiar as Mass to a Catholic or pantomime to an English child. The happy thunderous babel of voices washes over you like a sea.

"The dragon with the big claws," says a very small boy insistently. "Will the dragon be there like last year?"

"Betty!" cries one Cambridge mother to another, barely visible through the bobbing heads of her tribe. "I never see you except at the Revels!"

"Wouldn't be Christmas without it..."

"Daddy's going to sing the carols," says a small confident girl.

"You sing. I'll listen," says her lugubrious father through his overcoat collar.

The lights go down, the voices hush, and the families are deep suddenly in reawakened echoes of winter festivals from two thousand years past: pagan and Christian, Celtic and Nordic, Anglo-Saxon and Hebrew and a dozen other cultures. A clear solo voice sings the lilting Hebridean "Christ Child Lullaby;" eerily horned dancers stalk through a fertility dance as old as Stonehenge; in a bright swirl of medieval costume, a procession of musicians and chorus sings its way through the house to the stage. The dragon duly cavorts; beribboned Morris men leap and dance, a troupe of players brings brave Sir Gawain to challenge the Green Knight. The audience roars, laughs, sings, and at last finds itself winding in an immense dancing, singing line through the crowded lobby, led by a smiling dark-haired man whose voice rises strong over the rest:

> *Dance, then, wherever you may be,*
> *I am the Lord of the Dance, said he...*

And the lugubrious father is singing and dancing there too in the throng, overcoat flapping wide, a look of bemused delight on his face.

◆

We stand, John Meredith Langstaff and I, in the dim-lit theater among the empty seats, discussing a spring production of Revels. He waves at the air: "I want a great forty-foot mast to go up, in *Act One*, right here. Men hoisting it, singing sea chanties the way they were meant to be sung."

"That's lovely, but it's crazy. We'll hit that chandelier."

"There's some marvelous material — windlass chanties, chanties for hoisting sail..."

"Too dangerous. And what about the sight-lines?"

He says craftily; "We could have the mast sway, in that storm at the end of your seal story. Wouldn't that be great?"

"It won't work, Jack. We might brain half the audience. It'll be too heavy. Too complicated. Too —"

Three months later, a thousand people cheer as a tall shining mast rises dramatically on the stage of Sanders Theater, bringing timeworn sea chanties vividly alive. When the artistic director of the Revels has dreams, they tend to come true.

◆

Definitions of the Revels always sound terrible, like a biological description of the act of love. The Revels is not commercial theater; it isn't folksy; it isn't amateur; it isn't a concert – yet it combines certain strong elements from all these into a peculiar form of theatrical magic. The Christmas Revels company (which, like the script, is different each year) has a professional core but an amateur chorus. Each Revels blends song, dance, and drama into a celebration of the solstice. It is an answer to that submerged yearning for ritual, and for the marking of ancient landmarks in human life, which lies very deep in all of us and which very little in the American Way can satisfy. (In Britain that same yearning is probably the only reason why the monarchy survives.) Telling signs of emotion appear in letters from the fiercely possessive audiences who buy out every Revels production: "I can't remember the last time I felt such a personal involvement in a performance," ran a typical example one year. "I left with an incredible glow of joy."

John Langstaff, concert baritone and teacher, is the *onlie begetter* of the Revels; you might say he was born to it – on, suitably, Christmas Eve, into a family which always celebrated the winter solstice with a splendid singing party. He was always a singer, beginning as a choirboy at Grace Church in New York. He was always close to the English traditions which form a bulwark of all Revels programs; at fourteen he was playing St. George in a Country Dance and Song Society production of an old mummers' play. Friendships with May Gadd, Douglas Kennedy, Vaughn Williams, and other champions of English folk song and dance sealed his fascination with the early roots of the performing arts. By the time he reached the concert stage, he may have been the only classically trained singer in the United States who was also a skilled Morris dancer.

John Langstaff's first Christmas Revels was performed at Town Hall in New York City in 1956. A production in Washington followed, and then a televised Revels for NBC whose cast also included his daughter Carol, inheritor of similar talents and values. It was Carol who initiated the Cambridge series of the Revels in 1971.

Looking ahead, John Langstaff sounds more like a missionary than a performer or director: "There's this need – the lack of opportunity in people's lives to have any communal celebration. Remember Woodstock? That was a celebration of a kind, fed by the same need. What we try to do is to fill this gap that people feel but don't quite understand. We do it in two ways, I think: by the nature of the Revels material, which comes from things in their own cultural backgrounds that they can no longer remember or pass on to their children, and by getting them to participate. That's where the amateur chorus is important. The Revels has a core of professionals, yet the audience is able to feel part of it, not just through the sing-along element but by seeing people just like themselves up there on the stage so obviously having a good time. Given the right impetus, almost any community in America can develop a Revels tradition – college towns in particular have the mixture of professional and amateur talent built in. And the audience is always there, anywhere."

Community is a key word. There are child performers in every Revels production, and children make up a marvelously responsive part of all Revels audiences. But both audience and cast are necessarily cross sections of all the generations. The Revels, like folk song and folk tale, is for folk.

My own first sight of the Revels was a kind of magical shock; suddenly I was faced, in the theater, with the same myth-haunted world about which I'd been writing a sequence of books for the previous decade. John Langstaff, who has the unerring eye of a recruiting sergeant for Revels-oriented artists, had already noticed the link; as a result, I now find myself writing plays, verse, stories, lyrics, and any other words that a Revels production may require. Singers, musicians, producers, and actors all become involved in much the same way. "So-and-so is a Revels person," one says, as if discovering a hidden member of some special sect. Perhaps, somehow, this too communicates itself to the audience: the indefinable sense of a family at work.

For those involved in the making of the Revels, the year builds gradually up to Christmas. Ideas bubble; material from the encyclopedic Langstaff collection is sifted, chosen, rearranged. The familiar voice says at intervals on the telephone: "I've been having a few thoughts...."

Certain elements of the Christmas Revels program are more or less constant: carols in which the audience can join; Morris dances by one of two excellent New England teams, the Black Jokers or the Pinewoods Morris Men; a gripping choreographed version of "The Lord of the Dance," a song set by the Englishman Sydney Carter to the old Shaker hymn tune "Simple Gifts;" and variants of the traditional mummers' play St. George and the Dragon. In this blend of farce and gravity St. George, usually after most satisfyingly killing a large green dragon and/or a villainous Turkish knight, is – to the consternation of the younger members of the audience – himself killed by the pentangle of swords in a spectacular ritual dance. His subsequent resurrection, carrying with it endless echoes of the ancient, powerful myths of death and rebirth, is accomplished only by the magic and faith of the Fool – who, in assorted guises, is one of the haunting archetypal figures upon whom the "feel" of the Revels depends.

A devoted audience is a conservative animal, enjoying repetition. But the Revels, like St. George, must constantly renew itself in order to remain properly alive; so each program differs, in one way or another, from the one before. One Christmas Revels was set entirely in Victorian England, with street criers, waits, music-hall songs, a beautifully dressed house party, and "The Sorry Tale of Jacob Marley," a dramatized ghost story with all the Victorian stops pulled out. As far as we could tell, half the audience was disappointed by the lack of Morris Men, mummers, and medieval processionals and the other half was delighted, calling it "the best Revels ever." John Langstaff said cheerfully, "That's a healthy mix."

While the next Revels program evolves, a faithful production staff starts its work; professional artists are put under contract; auditions held for the amateur chorus; costumes, sets, props, and rehearsals planned and begun. The pattern then follows the nerve-racking crescendo of any piece of work in the theater, through the exultation of performance to the day, weeks later, when a group post-mortem is held over a video tape.

"The 'Alle Psallite' was better on the record."

"I'd like a French Revels, next year. Traditional, medieval. There's so much wonderful material."

"Terrific, we can make a huge stained-glass window. Or maybe we could project one on a cyc."

"And I'd like to use the Quadrivium, if they're free."

"You won't need me. There's this book I'm starting —"

"Oh. I thought you might like to rewrite the Gawain, in two parts. And maybe put the mummers into French."

"Now that would be fun...."

There aren't many limits to the power of Jack Langstaff's dream.

Getting to Revels

Gregory Maguire

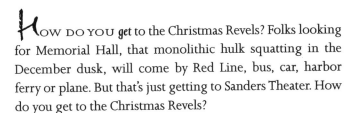

HOW DO YOU *get* to the Christmas Revels? Folks looking for Memorial Hall, that monolithic hulk squatting in the December dusk, will come by Red Line, bus, car, harbor ferry or plane. But that's just getting to Sanders Theater. How do you get to the Christmas Revels?

Revels is like a slow motion explosion. The force whirls around the stage and out from it, a feast for eyes, ears, the whole soul. You may find your family, friends and congregation there if you look. You get to Revels by the force of someone's enthusiasm, by the gift of a ticket, by following doctor's orders. Some folks get there just by accident; I think they're the lucky ones.

Six or seven years ago I got to Revels through a friend's double dare. "You like to sing? Here's an audition notice for the Revels chorus: two beers if you get up the nerve to try out!" So I did, weak in the knees but glad for the chance. The happy acceptance came in the mail shortly.

We launched into rehearsals, a handful of veterans and a larger number of novices. Even those of us who'd been to Revels performances couldn't imagine how our songs would segue into each other. "We'll sing **this**," John Langstaff coached us with sharp attention and unflagging bonhomie —"there'll be a little bit here we'll learn later, then we'll swing around and sing **that,** from here and here." Even those of us trained in flow charts, complex equations or scrimmage strategies couldn't quite picture it. Opening night grew perilously close, and "Oh, that transition! We'll learn that next week!" roared Jack. The veteran members of the chorus stayed calm. We novices sweated even though the weather grew steadily colder.

How do you get to the Christmas Revels? Well, you get there by a movement in your heart, a sort of involuntary lurch that sets you leaning toward light and movement and music in the darkest part of the year.

This winter marks the second year I am dragging along a couple of nephews to Revels. Six years since I sang in the chorus; maybe it's ten years since I first showed up alone, for medicinal purposes. The great thing is this: I still don't know, any more than my nephews do, what all this is about.

Every night for a week I stood on the stage and watched the Mummers' Play, which ended with the cry, "Dance, men, the Sword Dance now for me!" Every night the Morris Men sliced and leaped their dangerous way through the thicket of swords, and the hexagonal emblem of interlocked weapons was brandished aloft. Every night the swords were withdrawn, and the hapless youth crumpled to the stage floor. The audience gasped, though they knew it must come to this.

Every night I gasped too. Each night it seemed more and more tragic, and wonderful, and each night I understood less and less about how it worked, or why: each night I got closer to Revels.

The closer you get to Revels, the less you can know about it. The youth will rise and be reborn, and no reason in the world suffices. If Revels is the dance of life, pure and simple, it's also Mystery, even simpler. Getting to Revels. It's a lifelong process.

That's how you get to Revels. And getting back?

But whoever would want to?

Some Elements of Revels

John Langstaff

TRADITIONAL RITUAL, including ritual songs, dance and drama, has always been central to Revels. We've worked hard to maintain the integrity of the authentic rituals we've incorporated, of which there have been many: the antler dance from the village of Abbots Bromley, a traditional sword dance from Yorkshire, the *Bal do Sabre* from Italy and the *Calasari* from Romania. There have been women's waulking songs from the Hebrides, the Scots First Footing with its Hogmanay skin, Mexican Day of the Dead processions, the Santa Lucia celebration of young Swedish girls, the Soul-Cake ritual for All Hallows' Eve, seasonal folk plays of the traditional mummers or guisers, and the character of the shamanistic Folk Fool himself. Revels has been fortunate in finding extraordinary "tradition bearers" who've been critical in helping us maintain the power of those rituals. And we've been lucky enough to have a number of them join us on stage. We've welcomed Dmitri Pokrovsky bringing us Russian folk tradition, Norman Kennedy bringing us Celtic, Joseph Bruchac with Native American, Benoit Bourque with French Canadian, Bessie Jones from the Georgia Sea Islands, and Jean Ritchie from the Kentucky Mountains – to name just a few.

Over the decades, Revels' own traditions (or "rituals") have unknowingly evolved quite naturally. The audience anticipates *Lord of the Dance*, leaping from their seats to join hands with performers, singing and dancing out into the hall. A thousand voices combine in wonderful harmony, singing *Dona Nobis Pacem*. We have the great communal shout of "Welcome Yule!" at the end of Susan Cooper's poem, *The Shortest Day*. And always there's our finale with brass and everyone in the hall singing *The Sussex Mummers' Carol*. These have become Revels rituals. And what makes for the ritual? Certainly **expectancy** is part of it; our audiences have come to expect these elements in Revels. For our part, we cherish their expectancy. It helps create the ritual.

I'm often asked, "How do you get a crowd to sing with you?" My answer is simple. You lead them with the same energy you expect from them. The absolute assurance that they **will** sing helps make it happen. Singing from the audience is an integral part of Revels. But a "sing-along" Revels is not: we script those moments when an audience sings as carefully as we script our most virtuoso solo performance moments.

Most of all, Revels depends on something communal, connective. It comes out of the material we choose and the deep commonality of ancient ritual that is felt, even if not spelled out or explicitly understood. It comes also from the participation we engage, both within the audience itself and between our audience and performers on stage. Somewhere in that connectedness is the real magic of a Revels performance.

The Ploughman & the Concert Artist: Alasdair Fraser

Elizabeth Lloyd Mayer

THE RUDDY FACE was familiar, but it took me a moment to place it. Then I saw the fiddles. Of course – Alasdair Fraser, among the finest traditional Scottish fiddlers alive today. He'd performed in our 1992 California Christmas Revels. A consummate artist, he walked on stage and the show caught fire.

Courtesy of United Airlines, we were now seated next to each other on a packed 747, the 12-hour non-stop from London to San Francisco. Alasdair turned to me: familiar shy grin, thick Scots speech, eager intensity I remembered wonderfully well. "You know," he said, "I never told you what performing in Revels meant to me."

The plane took off. And so did Alasdair. At a certain point, I grabbed a pen and started taking furious notes. Did he mind, I asked? "Mind? No, no," he said. "When I talk, I find words. When I write, I don't – put it all down."

This is some of what I put down.

●

I'll tell you about Revels and what it was for me. It's about the ploughman who feels the plough in his hands and about the concert artist who soars and tastes that nectar. Both. Together. Revels makes a place for both because both are needed to make the real music, the joy that's pure, unadulterated, that's life at its loftiest.

That's what I live for and it's why Revels is more than Revels. Revels is a torch, a touchstone that's very rare. It's the people. They're kindred spirits. They carry torches of community and sharing and passion. If I detect that passion, I immediately know I'm going to burn hotter as an artist. Revels made me burn as I'd rarely burned....

My challenge in this life is to be rooted in tradition, in the deepest grass roots. But the real challenge is also to soar. Those two things are very hard to do together. It's incredibly difficult to soar to capacity in nuance and art, but also be deeply, solidly rooted in the soil. Revels does both in a way I've rarely found elsewhere. Revels is an open embrace, an inclusiveness, a commitment to abundance rather than scarcity, to the non-defensive posture in life...

Revels is bigger than Revels. It's a jumping-off point for people. The Solstice is just the beginning. Revels is about what life should be about: raising the ceiling of life on a daily basis. But we have to fight to get rid of the tight defensiveness that holds people down...

I do daft things like getting bureaucrats, funders, everyone, to step-dance: in huge meetings, thousands of people, political meetings. First I play. Then after I've played, I say, "If you go back to your life now, you'll be unhealthy with this energy. You have to vent it for your health, all this energy you've absorbed." Because I feel it in them. And then they come alive...

Or I will have audiences drone. They become part of a great sound, a huge bagpipe. I'll play an ancient chant over their drone. And I'll know we've gone somewhere because they won't stop. I'll stop and they won't. They can't stop because they're so involved with each other and the sound they're making with my sound. My sound rises over theirs, under theirs, it's one. They stop living dampened down when that happens...

We can take great artists and put them on stage for 2000 people and they know how to soar. But they need the tradition-bearers, the ones who know what the plough feels like in the hand, the horse underneath them. People need both for true nourishment. Tradition-bearers won't hold a large audience; that isn't what they know how to do. So each needs the other...

Once a woman came up to me in a coffee shop and said, "You're Alasdair Fraser, aren't you?" I said, "Yes." And she said, "My daughter has a terrible illness and she's 12. Last year, the doctors needed to operate but because her blood pressure was so low, they wouldn't. And I said to the doctors, 'But when my daughter hears certain music she comes alive. Most of all that happens with a CD called Skyedance by Alasdair Fraser. See what happens when you play it.' And they did. Her blood pressure went up, so they kept playing it and decided they could operate. They played it through the whole surgery. The doctors couldn't believe it."...

I love the beauty in mathematics, in physics, but it's the same beauty that's in the music of the old ploughmen or that made the girl's blood pressure rise. Beauty is a big word. It's not to be thrown off easily. It's in the leap you'd never predict: it's in the leap that's the essence of life, where creativity happens. It's in the zone of your head where you await response, a zone of not knowing...

I used to be a physicist — I know, hard to believe! After university I worked for an oil company, working at how the hell you figure out where oil is under the sea. Only after seven years of it did I realize science could become art. I'd hang out all night in bars with old guys, cigarettes sticking out of their mouths. They'd say "Dig here." I'd say, "Why?" They'd say they just knew. It was art. Slowly I learned. It didn't come out of anything I'd been taught as a scientist....

I'd been taught art was a luxury. It's not. The art of those men got me to where I finally hit escape velocity. That's when the penny dropped. I thought: there's no one in the world not affected by music. And I realized: so it's not a luxury. It's not an add-on. The next day, I quit the oil company. And I've been a fiddler ever since...

Revels is a celebration of the leap. That's where the source of Revels is. What leap? Into life? Maybe into the hero's journey; something like that. The safety-loving world will tell you to make a list of pros and cons about life. But the leap is where life lives. It's the leap into oneness. Revels isn't spiritual, yet it is spiritual. At least, I would like to think Revels has a high knowledge, which is the relationship of life to oneness....

We need a platform for that, for the expression of it. It's what the tradition-bearers know. The result for them is a deep knowing of life. High language doesn't capture the leap. Revels tries to give people that platform — give it to people who aren't on the plough, give them a taste of what it feels like, a taste of the leap into life, a leap into oneness....

Bring Revels to Scotland! We need it. Strange, isn't it: here I am living in California, knowing how we've lost that soul and need to bring it back to Scotland. New Year's in Glasgow: hogmanay on the telly and getting bashed and that's it. It's desperate and sad. We need Revels, we really do.

◆

The plane is well over the Atlantic by now. I've been writing steadily as we've talked, grabbing phrases that particularly caught me. Alasdair looks straight at me. "You know the thing about this conversation? There's been no noise. There you are: that's Revels."

From the Wings

Katherine Fiveash

IN THE THEATER the lights have dimmed and the audience settles in the dark, waiting. We stand in our costumes, feeling cold drafts from the December night flood the huge, empty space of Memorial Hall's transept. In just over an hour, after the first act, a multitude of people will swirl into this space to dance with us. As the brass begins to play, we silently enter the hall, and our lives fall away from us. We are teachers, students, secretaries, doctors, engineers, carpenters, computer programmers. But for this moment we become a new community, a village in another place and another time. We have invented for ourselves families, occupations and histories; we are shepherds and weavers, farmers and fishermen, brewers and cobblers and midwives. We have come together to find comfort and joy in the darkest time of the year. The power of the Solstice pulses in the theater as the music begins; our hearts feel that pulse and beat with its ancient rhythm. Our months of rehearsing are ended as we join our audience and start to sing, moving through the aisles towards the stage.

The energy coming from the audience feels like a force of nature. It magnifies us, makes us respond with joy. There is a mutuality of experience among audience members and performers, among professionals and volunteers, that is quintessentially Revels. It unites us with generations of people who have gathered in the dead of winter to ward off the forces of darkness with ritual, music and comradeship. Our singing and dancing call up that vast history of human celebration embedded in our collective memory.

But being a chorus member in Revels is not just about collective memory and universal human experience. It also has its intensely personal aspects. As the series of performances gathers momentum, certain parts of each show become touchstones for me. A story that I hear over and over on stage penetrates my life and becomes a way for me to understand my own experience. Singing a particular song opens a closed place in my heart. When the dancers create their remarkable illusion of deer in the Abbots Bromley Horn Dance, I remember in a visceral way my connection to the natural world. As I watch the Mummers' Play each night, the inexorable moment of death in the sword dance and the magical rebirth of St. George represent a profound truth. Performance after performance, the mysteries of light and darkness, death and rebirth, scarcity and abundance, frivolity and wisdom, deepen for me.

Perhaps that duality captures something essential about Revels. We need opportunities like this for the universal to penetrate our personal lives. Audience members come to Revels to celebrate, sing, and be entertained, but also perhaps to be reminded of connections to ancient human fears, hopes and traditions. Chorus members come to be part of a community of people who work in the theater. But at the same time, they forge another link in the long chain of human activities that have marked the Solstice season for so many years in so many cultures. Now in midwinter, when the year is at its lowest ebb, we pause together to reflect on the cyclic nature of life. In doing that we find renewal. We experience the rebirth of light and hope on earth – and in our hearts.

The Appeal of "Revelry by Night"

The Rev. George Blackman

My FIRST CHRISTMAS REVELS? How well I remember it! The day itself had not put any of us in a festive mood. It was one of those cloudy, windless ones that chill the heart as well as the blood, with temperatures hovering around freezing.

So it was a fretful family who, grumbling about overcrowding and bruised toes, piled into the car for Cambridge and then trudged through freezing slush towards Memorial Hall. Spirits did not lift much when we got inside. The hallway was cold, damp, noisy and crowded, lit bleakly by chandeliers.

Once we got to our seats we relaxed…but only a bit. Small children were twisting about in their seats and asking a stream of unanswerable questions. Their elders looked frowningly at programs (which on this occasion contributed still further to a newcomer's nervousness by warning that far from sitting passively all evening while the Revels company sang its heart out, the audience would have to do some singing too).

Suddenly the lights dimmed. There was a wave of whispering, quickly hushed. On the balcony above the stage, a brass ensemble began to play. Out of the darkness came a sound of singing, far off but drawing nearer. As the lights sprang up again, from every entrance came a line of men, women and children in mediæval costumes, singing the opening carol. They were in front of us, behind us, seeming almost as numerous as the audience itself. As they passed, something extraordinary began to happen. It was as if each line carried a thread that wove everyone sitting there into one all-encompassing pattern. By the time the actors gathered to face us, the stage had somehow expanded to include us all. What began as a theatrical performance had mysteriously become a celebration which turned a company of strangers into what felt like one vast extended family. Then and there the Revels became as integral to our own family Christmas as the annual candlelight carol service in our home church or presents under the tree. We haven't missed one since. Each year we drive home arguing the merits of the most recent Revels, like connoisseurs comparing successive vintages of a favorite wine.

Part of the perennial appeal of Revels is easy enough to identify. The songs and dances have interest and charm in themselves. A production that makes room for the disciplined expertise of the professional as well as the enthusiastic energy of the amateur, has the best of both worlds. And there is something wonderful about an evening in which three generations mingle happily on stage, unencumbered by hearty attempts to treat adults like over-sized children or children like pint-sized adults.

However, I think the appeal of the Revels goes much deeper. The Revels manage to reconnect us with ethnic roots severed when our forebears (whoever they were) left their Old Worlds (wherever they happened to be). The Revels stage is not always a mediæval English hall. Sometimes it is a Russian steppe, an Appalachian clearing, a Cornish quay, a Victorian drawing room or the dooryard of a Southern cabin (for me, among the most memorable was that dooryard when it was presided over by the unmistakable majesty of the late

Bessie Jones). The effect of all this variety is fascinating. It doesn't set people apart. It brings them together. Partly that's because of the welcoming spirit in which the Revels are performed. This is no museum rite from which you feel excluded if you don't have the requisite ethnic genes. Whatever your own ethnic roots, you find yourself putting down fresh ones in the Revels, wherever the soil seems to suit. And that is a rare and invigorating experience.

I suspect that the central theme of the Revels is also a crucial aspect of why it brings people so powerfully together. Whether we gather to commemorate the shortest or longest day of the year, what we are acknowledging is the duality that profoundly shapes earthly existence: an existence in which light and darkness complement and also oppose each other. In that light and dark we experience life and death, love and indifference, the wholeness of health and the disintegration of disease.

When I first joined hands with the person next to me to find I was following the Revels cast out of the theatre during *Lord of the Dance*, I was surprised to discover that I was very deeply moved. Despite the happy faces and gaiety of the music, there was something else: something solemn, at once courageous and heart-rendingly vulnerable about that coiling line. Long afterwards, reading an article about the labyrinths commonly placed at the western end of mediæval cathedrals or traced in the turf of ancient fields, I think I understood why. Unwittingly, we had been dancing in the footsteps of our ancestors, treading together that labyrinthine way which leads out of darkness into light.

In the solstice ritual, the passions that daily set human beings against each other pale before the towering mystery of Light and Dark, now advancing, now retiring, in a dance

whose meaning is beyond human control or human com-
prehension. It is a dance which humans can only hope to
dance by dancing together. That is the experiential truth
which does indeed transform the Revels audience and cast
into a great bonded unit of humanity. For a moment at least,
we do become one family, together touching the essence of
life.

The Engines of Our Ingenuity

John H. Lienhard

TODAY, we become children for an evening. The University of Houston's College of Engineering presents this series about **machines** that make our civilization run, and the **people** whose ingenuity created them.

I've just been to a new kind of theatre. It's called The Revels. The Revels began in Boston. Now it's spreading from one American city to another. The format is close to vaudeville. It's a loosely connected set of folk themes, music, recitations, dance, and skits. They all revolve around some ancient ceremonial theme like the Summer or Winter Solstice.

It's a lot of fun; but what arrests me is the way it satisfies a craving. The belief that we can find truth by utterly rational means has dealt us false. We've laid every aspect of life under our microscopes. Yet those microscopes never **did** offer to show us what life is all about.

Now we see that we've lost a whole piece of understanding ourselves by ignoring the old folk stories and myths. You've heard Joseph Campbell on that theme. Well, he has good company. Child psychologist Bruno Bettelheim, tells about fairy tales. He says we can only wring meaning from life by courageously struggling against what seem to be overwhelming odds. This is the message that fairy tales get across to children. Struggle is unavoidable and intrinsic. Only if we don't shy away; only if we steadfastly meet unexpected and unjust hardship, can we overcome obstacles and emerge victorious.

Modern children's stories avoid these problems. Yet children badly need to hear, in *symbolic* form, how to deal with them. *Safe* stories don't mention death, aging, the limits to our existence, nor the wish for eternal life. *Fairy tales* confront children squarely with these parts of the basic human predicament.

Robert Bly recently looked at the problem of male isolation in our society. He reads us the Grimms' fairy tale of *Iron John*. He explains its clear and very wise instructions on how to turn a boy into a man. We've grown too clever to hear the succinct wisdom of this old fairy tale. Now, too many American men are unfinished. We resort to addiction, brutality, or retreat, to push away the pain of our incompleteness.

So the Revels audience dances out of the theatre onto the greensward. We all sing about uniting our separated souls, of climbing the hills to pull wild mountain thyme. We meet the healing folk mythology for a moment, on a very special level.

It's a peculiar moment. It's a moment when we acknowledge that, to be whole, we must serve the head with a full range of hearing. It's a moment peculiar to *any* creative process. It's a moment when we once again find truth by gazing at the world with the eyes of a child.

(*KUHF Broadcast #558, June 1991*)

The Mummers' Play

Patrick Swanson

THE TYPICAL MUMMERS' PLAY opens with a "calling on" in which one of the performers clears a space, craves the audience's indulgence and promises a fine performance. This over, the two protagonists appear, and after each has done his share of boasting and established his bravery, they engage in a fight. In the duel, one of them is wounded or killed. A Doctor is then summoned and after lengthily establishing his credentials and healing skills, administers all manner of outlandish medicines to revive the fallen hero. Sometimes the Doctor fails, and the Fool takes over, using a sprig of evergreen or mistletoe to bring the dead man back to life (evergreen having magic powers because it stays green in winter and mistletoe because it fruits in the snow and has no roots in the earth). Here the main business of the play ends. At this point, various minor characters enter and provide a little simple entertainment after which one of them collects money, and the performance ends with a song.

The collection of a fee strengthens the notion that the Mummers are performing a service and bringing good luck to the community. The theatrical death and rebirth associated with the dying off of the old year and the birth of the new is deadly serious, a ritual at the core of human experience, but the Mummers perform their play in a broad and crudely comic style. When we asked the Armagh Rhymers (an Irish mumming troupe from the Northern Counties) for advice on how to perform Mummers' Plays, their suitably paradoxical answer was, "Get on fast, say your lines fast, and get off fast. Because it doesn't mean anything at all. (Laughter.) Or does it?"

The Mummers' Play is probably the oldest of all performances. The word "mumming" may be derived from the German *mummen* – a mask, or the French *momer* – to act in dumb show. "Keeping mum" is English vernacular for staying silent. Performed in certain English towns and villages, the play is often attached to a folk or ritual dance. Whatever may have been its past, it now has very few of the qualities that are associated with drama. There is no continuous linking of events leading up to and away from a crisis, no dramatic tension or psychological interplay of characters. Yet the roots of theater are inextricably tangled with those of ritual and primitive religion, and the Mummers' Play, crude and undeveloped as it may be, bears distinct traces of its ritual origin.

A prehistoric cave painting in the Dordogne region of France depicts a human figure dressed in the skins and horns of a deer-like animal. Human eyes are peering through the mask formed by the animal's head – a ritual moment, and perhaps the first recorded act of theater. This image has an uncanny similarity to the costume and attitude of the dancers in the Abbots Bromley Horn Dance. In the English town of Abbots Bromley, ten performers go down to the church to receive the costumes and the six sets of reindeer horns required for the Horn Dance. Following the procession of six dancers who carry the huge horns are four supernumeraries – the Fool, Hobby-Horse, Maid Marion and Boy-Archer. These mysterious characters from a forgotten play have no lines; their action is to follow the dancers in silence and to keep "mum." Local explanations and descriptions of the dance emphasize the idea of a deer hunt, but many of the local farm workers whose villages are visited by the dancers link it to fertility rites. "*It's a queer do,*" a local farmer is noted as commenting, "*but we would have bad luck if they missed us out.*"

The original Mummers' Play may have had a precise function. In primitive cultures there was a conviction, well known to anthropologists, that you could make things happen by doing them yourself – sticking pins in the wax effigy of an enemy to cause him injury, or melting the effigy over a fire to hasten his death. In some tribes a representative of the spirit of life would be put through a pretended death and then restored to life. An offshoot of this conviction was the idea of a conflict between the old year and the new, of the waxing and the waning of life on earth. This theme is ritualized in the Mummers' Play.

The English director Peter Brook who (with his group of international actors in France) has been researching theater and theater audiences for over thirty years, observes in non-classical world theater a correlation between ritual *gravitas* and roughness of acting style. The emphasis is on what is being done, not in how they are doing it. In Revels, the Mummers' Play is a boisterous affair often delivered by a mix of amateur and professional actors. This irreverent and comic vehicle transports the audience towards an unusual moment: when the hero falls dead, he marks the symbolic death of the old year. The Revels audience – who are gathered both to be entertained and to celebrate together at this special time of the year – are, perhaps unknowingly, on the threshold of contemporary ritual. One of the characteristics of ritual is repetition. The English folklorist Cecil Sharp was intrigued by local folk dances and plays which were performed in villages and handed on from one generation to another. To the question *"Why do you perform?"* the answer was often, *"Because my father did it that way."* The community looked forward to seeing the same dance or play done by a new generation in more or less the way their elders handed it on to them. The meaning of the old lines or dance steps might be obscure, but it was important to the village or town to continue the tradition, and to add the present experience to that of their ancestors, in some way accumulating significance. Audiences who have participated in early Revels shows display a similar tendency. After thirty years, there are families who have several generations of exposure to Revels; they value the experience as a family ritual. Certainly there are elements in the Revels that have more or less ritual possibilities – the *"Lord of the Dance,"* which ends the first act of every show, joins actors and audience in dance and song. Spilling from the stage to the lobby, the dance gathers more and more participants, blurring the divide between those who are doing and those who are watching. Finally the lobby is filled and the dance ends with a communal shout. However ephemeral this sense of communitas, we could do worse than exercise the muscles that help it to happen. The old lines given to the willing victim in the Mummers' Play focus the human mystery that brings us all together:

> First comes Christmas, then comes Spring.
> Like Winter I must die. Then to life again like Spring.

The Abbots Bromley Horn Dance

Douglas Kennedy, O.B.E.

AMONG THE SURVIVING RITUAL DANCES in the calendar of English folk customs, none is more surprising than the Abbots Bromley ceremony of "deer-running." I first saw the Horn Dance in the streets of Abbots Bromley in about 1920. As the local traffic gave way with patient resignation, the policeman explained, "It's an old custom believed to bring good luck, representing a deer hunt of long ago."

Many years later when I watched the ceremony, it left the town and took to the lanes leading to neighboring farms. I asked a farmer, "Do you mind this annual invasion of your fields and stockyards?"

"Mind!" he said, "On the contrary, we should be anxious indeed if we were left out; we would fear for our harvest and the lambing."

While the local records of the Horn Dance go back 500 years or more, there are suggestions that similar dance processions were already old before Europe became Christian. Discoveries of rock paintings in caves hollowed out in the limestone of the Dordogne Valley in France and elsewhere indicate that the Horn Dance may even trace its origin among hunting tribes in the "Europe" of 20,000 to 50,000 years ago.

The costumes and other properties of the Abbots Bromley Horn Dance, including the six sets of reindeer antlers, were always housed in the Church porch until recently, and each year the first "running" is made in front of the Church. The attitude of the resident parson towards this local folk custom has, through the years, varied considerably, but it has usually been tolerated for its ancient tradition despite its admittedly pagan origin.

The dance has two formations: first, the serpentine procession, single file, during which the head of the "serpent" can turn back on itself, ravel, then unravel without halting the progress. The whole "snake" requires ten actors or dancers: six "deer" with antlers and four motley characters – Fool, Hobby-Horse, Maid Marion and Boy-Archer. The antlers are held up so that each deer-man can salute, threaten or bow low. The second part of the Horn Dance is in a set formation of two lines, with Archer and Maid Marion opposite Horse and Fool. The lines meet and retire three times, then pass through to resume their serpentine procession.

The Fool is a medicine man, a maker of magic, and the oldest "actor," a universal in folk custom. Hobby-Horse, who follows Fool, is a totem animal-man. Maid Marion, another widely-spread folk character, is really the "woman-man," the complete human being in Mother guise. Boy-Archer is the universal hunter who, through the ages, has sought some means of making his apologies to the animals he has pursued and killed in order to survive.

The need for humans to make religion or myth of their dread of becoming separated from the animals and plants is illustrated by widespread relics and ancient rites, some of which survive as folk dramas and ritual dances with universal folk characters like these four. Like fossils found in rocks, even though compressed and fragmentary, these surviving relics and rites have their illuminating story to tell.

In a series of caves discovered by three boys in 1914 and

named *Les Trois Frères*, there are great networks of galleries showing different animals, all in lively motion, depicted at least 20,000 years ago. The largest figure shows a man in disguise with human legs and feet, great antlers on his head. Who is he? The Abbé Breuil, accepted authority on the cave paintings, called him the "Sorcerer," a maker of magic. He might have served as a decoy to bring animals nearer to hunters, but the Abbé thinks it more likely that he represents the First Actor, the Animal-Man preserving the link between Human Being and Nature. He is portrayed in the act of dancing.

Cecil Sharp, when he published his description of the deer-dance, called it a "processional" and put it among his Sword Dances of Northern England, since they too had fragments of drama in the characters of Fool and Betty (man-woman), and since the Sword Dance figures were the prime maze-makers with their almost incredible raveling and unraveling.

Sharp, who collected so many fine tunes with the Cotswold Morris Dances, regretted that there were no comparable folk tunes for the Horn Dance. Some years after his publication of the Horn Dance, he received by post from an elderly cleric a manuscript copy of a tune titled "The Horn Dance Tune." This gentleman had connection with Abbots Bromley and knew the local man who had noted the music. Sharp immediately published the tune. He himself thought it lovely, but the local dancers and musicians rejected it as wrong for the dance the way they locally performed it. When I suggested to Sharp in 1920 the idea of trying to make the dance fit the tune, Sharp said to me, "*I wish you would have a go and try it out.*" So we set to.

We worked out the dance as described in Sharp's book with its helpful diagrams for spacing and direction, and showed it at Cheltenham College in a very high Gothic room, with long lancet windows, dimly lit by the twilight of a fading summer. Our lead fiddler, Elsie Avril, started playing the haunting Horn Dance tune outside, and then led us on. Our steps and manner of progress dictated by the new tune were rather different from the casual-looking jogtrot of the local performance to popular tunes. The immediate effect of our entry was to set an atmosphere of magic and mystery. We ourselves, raptly concentrating on our spacing and changes of direction, were caught up in a web of our own spinning. For myself as the lead stag, I felt more than half-stag, swinging my antlers and snorting to signal the changes in the dance formation. Until this performance began we had little idea of a style, but we quickly discovered how the antlers seemed to take charge of us as we ducked and half-shied while we tied our apparent knots in the magical snaking thread. By the time we felt we had done justice to the occasion and I signaled to the fiddler to follow us off, we knew we had woven a spell over a semi-stunned audience. When the lights went up, we found not a few in tears, including the great man himself. "I knew," he said, "the tune was magic, but I had no idea what it might do to the dance."

Our interpretation has not had any effect whatever on the down-to-earth reality of the local tradition, which continues as of yore. For Revels and other occasions of artistic license, the "new tune" (or perhaps it should be called the "old tune") can have its own place.

The Horn Dance may be just another fossil relic of antiquity but it is still charged with the old mystery, and I have no doubt myself that the old tune has the power to spill some extra magic out of the Animal-Man's haversack.

The Long Sword Dances of England

John Bremer

THE SWORD DANCES from England are not national dances. They were found in England, and the English preserved them, but they are exemplars of a human, pan-world ritual, and it is only by good fortune that some of the best examples were found in England.

They were discovered by Cecil Sharp who, beginning in 1910, collected fourteen dances, all published in his three-part *Sword Dances of Northern England*. Most of the dances had not been performed for more than twenty years and Sharp saved them from extinction by tracking down individual dancers and musicians.

The dances were of two kinds: first, the Long Sword Dances, which used a sword about 29 inches long, with a wooden hilt of about 5 inches. Some swords were of stiff steel, without sharp edges, and about one inch wide; others were made of wood. There were either 6 or 8 dancers, always men. Second, the Short Sword Dances, usually referred to as *rapper* sword, were performed with a flexible blade of about 24 inches, with a swiveling handle at one end and a flat wooden grip at the other. These dances were performed by a team of 5 men. The Long Sword Dances are undoubtedly older. (One other dance Sharp collected was from Flamborough, on the coast of the North Sea, but it was properly an implement or tool dance, the "sword" being carried in the left hand, with the figures imitating the intricate making of fishing nets. It is usually classified as a Long Sword Dance.)

The Sword Dance was performed after the Winter Solstice, the shortest day of the year. The connection with the earth is indicated by a common name given to many of the dances – "Plough Stots," "stot" being Old English for a young ox (which pulled the plough). Plough Monday, when many teams danced, was the first Monday following Twelfth Night. Ploughing resumed following Twelfth Night; although called "the twelve days of Christmas," the holiday was originally pagan and was co-opted by Christianity.

Originally, the Long Sword Dance was accompanied by a play, fragments of which have been preserved. The plot was invariable – representing the conflict of dark and light, evil and good, death and resurrection. The names of the characters in the play vary from place to place and time to time, depending partly on the current religious or political situation, but the outcome is always the re-birth of St. George or whoever is currently the representative of the good.

St. George may die, but he is brought back to life (as the earth is brought back to life) by a magical agency – a kind of medicine man, often with the title of Fool (or, more properly, Mr. Fool). The death and resurrection of the play is represented in the culmination of each of the several parts (or figures) of the Long Sword Dance, five or six figures being the common number.

The dancers link up into a "hilt-and-point ring" and dance most of the Sword Dance so joined. The step is a steady and rhythmical dance-walk, which can accelerate into a run at climactic moments, but the experience of the dance for me (and I have danced and taught Long Sword for more than sixty years) is the eternal circling to a steady beat, in company with other men, which produces an incredible image of eternity; the team is at one with the circle or cycle of the universe.

· ⚔⚔

After the circlings and cross-circlings, the movements of single- and double-, under- and over- and the like, the side (as the team is called) forms a shape of interwoven swords: a six- or eight-pointed star. The star is raised by Number One, the leader of the side, at the end of each figure, while the whole set dances round at an increasing tempo. This "nut" or "knot" or "lock" is then lowered down so that each man can grasp the hilt of a sword; in doing this, the hole in the center of the lock is put over the head of the character – the St. George of the moment or Mr. Fool – and the swords, when drawn in the final bar, symbolically decapitate him. (Perhaps, once, it was not merely symbolic.) In the play, he is then brought back to life.

The Long Sword Dance is the expression of a community's acceptance of its dependence on the bountiful (if uncontrollable) cycle of nature, the eternal round of life-death-resurrection. Even if we do not understand or accept the theology that may have accompanied this – and the villagers for whom the dance was done probably didn't understand it either – we can feel the unity with the natural cycle. That is its perfection.

It would appear that the Long Sword Dances all belong in the region around the ancient city of York. Around 900 A.D. this region was occupied by the Danes or Vikings, in an area called either Danish Mercia or the Danelagh. We do not know whether the Long Sword Dances came with the Danes or not, but the geographical and historical connection is certainly highly suggestive.

Furthermore, while the Saxons invaded England (400–750 A.D.) from northern Europe before the Danes arrived (800–900 A.D.), both Saxons and Danes had a common ancestry (although they probably did not know it, and undoubtedly wouldn't have cared if they had). This commonality was to be found in the indo-European peoples who had been spreading both east and west from an area near the Caspian Sea since 3000 B.C.E. It is quite probable that they brought with them their ritual dances – the Cotswold Morris with the Saxons, and the Long Sword with the Danes. One thing is certain: the Cotswold Morris and the Long Sword have a common root somewhere in their history, and before they arrived in England. They are both circular nature dances, although the Morris has moved further away from the common origin than the Sword Dance.

Notes on the Green Man

Patrick Swanson

As a child growing up in England, I was always attracted to stories about Robin Hood and his outlaw band. Robin's men dressed in Lincoln green. They gave up on civilization and took to the woods, the better to conduct a novel social experiment in which they gave to the poor what they stole from the rich. In London alone, there are over thirty pubs called "The Green Man," many of which feature Robin Hood on their inn signs.

There is, however, a wilder and altogether more mysterious fellow who goes by the name of Green Man. Displacing jaunty, clean-shaven Robin, he appears on pub signs as a male head disgorging vegetation from his mouth, and sometimes from his eyes and ears. This foliate version of the Green Man I found strangely familiar. And no wonder. Once I began to look for him, I found him all around me. I saw him chiseled into pediments in churches, supporting statues of the virgin, carved into the beam of a Suffolk barn, and hammered into Victorian guttering. He appeared on the wrought iron gates of Kew Gardens, at the base of cathedral spires, even on the door knocker of my local bank. Like Robin Hood (or Robin-of-the-Wood as he used to be known), he is a forest creature. His face peers through the leaves, confirming our sense of the woods and the natural world as wakeful and alive. Even in our most civilized surroundings, we wonder at the blade of grass that somehow finds its way through the concrete. This leafy Green Man, a descendent of the vegetation or nature god, evokes a quality of irrepressible life. In a tradition that appears universal across cultures, human beings have ritualized his death and resurrection to mirror the animal death and rebirth of Nature.

In a similar vein, the central episode of traditional folk plays and sword dances performed in village festivals throughout England and Europe is a mock beheading or slaying of a heroic figure or Fool, followed by a revival or restoration of life. The most obvious English folk relative of the Green Man goes by the name of Jack-in-the-Green. Portrayed as a tower of leaves crowned by flowers, he is escorted by dancers dressed in green tatters as he capers through the many dances of annual May festivals. During the last dance of the day, the dancers drive their wooden swords into the leaves of his covering; the crowd cheers and Jack-in-the-Green falls over dead. The ritual is complete and will be repeated the following year. The spirit of summer has been released.

In the epic poem, *Gawain and the Green Knight* (turned into a brief play-within-a-play for performance in our French-Norman Christmas Revels), it is the figure of the Green Knight who interrupts King Arthur's Christmas Feast and demands to have his head cut off as part of a Christmas game. After the beheading comes the story of a year's heroic quest and the Green Knight's eventual resurrection.

Whether as Green Knight, Jack-in-the-Green, King of the May, my old hero Robin or the Green Man of antiquity – in all his characterizations, he is a figure who brings fundamental knowledge with him: the assurance and the deep race memory that inexhaustible life is stored within the roots of the world, even in the dead of winter. The Green Man tells us to live in perpetual expectation of the unexpected if we wish for a Spring rebirth.

The Revels and Folklore

Hugh M. Flick, Jr.

*T*HE REVELS are performances centered around the human need to celebrate. They provide an ongoing opportunity to experience – not just study, but actually experience – a wide variety of folkloric communications. Folklore has been defined in many different ways. At its essence, folklore is a communicative process used by members of affinity groups to express group identity, transmit group values, convey collective wisdom, and provide psychological strategies for coping with life. The worldview and belief structures of an affinity group will determine the format of that group's particular folklore. The Revels provide an opportunity to experience the vast range of culturally-specific folkloric communication, but they do it in a way that highlights certain underlying universals of what it means to be human.

People have inherent needs to celebrate. Those needs express themselves through various rituals and calendrical festivals. Celebrations and festivals occur at points of transition in the human life cycle (like marriages and puberty rituals) as well as at times that mark culturally significant cycles (like solar and lunar passages). They provide opportunities for affinity groups to offer guidance and reassurance to group members during the uncertainties and dangers of "liminal" periods, those times when ordinary boundaries shift and rules falter. They also provide occasions for individuals to release tensions and stress built up during non-festival periods.

In its "true folk" context, folklore is always a group activity. If there is performance involved, it is performed by group members for group members; distinctions between audience and performers are not hard and fast. The Revels are not "true folk" performances, but they do consciously maintain this haziness between audience and performers. The Revels are not just a passive experience for those who make up an audience. The audience is drawn into active participation with those on stage. So the audience is invited to sing with performers at certain moments. Performers often move through the audience or bring audience members up on stage or hand out some bit of food to those in the audience. During the intermission, the audience traditionally dances with the cast.

In my folklore classes at Harvard, I have found that the communicative nature of folklore is very difficult to present effectively in an academic setting. Lectures and textbooks simply cannot give students a genuine sense of what it's like to experience actual performance of the material. The study of folklore out of its performance context can be not only dry – worse, it can be misleading. Incorporating demonstrations, films, videotapes and recordings in my classes helps; I bring those in as much as possible. But I also strongly recommend that students attend Revels performances. The Revels offer something rare in our culture: a rich source for coming to appreciate the transformative power of folklore as it can be actually experienced, as it touches the heart, body, and soul, not just the mind.

Festivity and Spirituality

Harvey Cox

My THESIS is simply stated: the fiesta is just as religious as the pilgrimage; the dance is just as spiritual as the prayer. In fact for thousands of people for many millennia the festival *was* the main religious event in their lives. And mimic movement and ritual gesture were the principal ways of communicating with the holy.

We have lost some of this embodied feel for the sacred in our highly cognitive, productivity-oriented modern culture. But we have also lost something else. We have lost an invaluable source for resisting the forces that threaten to deprive us of our humanity.

The French historian Roger Chartier, writes:

> ... the festival is one of the privileged scenes where one may observe the popular resistance to normative injunctions as well as the restructuring, through cultural models, of the behavior of the majority.

What Chartier means is that the festival is not just a playground. It is also a battleground. It is the *circus maximus* where symbolic forces contend, the continuing Agincourt where the socially powerful groups in any society seek to tame the energies and enlist the allegiance of those they seek to rule.

I did not grow up in one of the pre-modern French villages that Roger Chartier writes about. I came from a small Pennsylvania town dominated by a steel tubing factory. Still, I think I know what he means. In the little Pennsylvania town I grew up in we had no saints' days, but we did have the annual Fire Company Fair, and no one who grew up there will ever forget it. It was a two-week carnival that combined gambling wheels and refreshment stands provided by the local volunteer firemen and the women's auxiliary, with a Ferris wheel and side-show supplied by a traveling road company. This all went on in a town where gambling was technically illegal and there was none – at least in the open – the other fifty weeks of the year. During the Fire Company Fair, however, the whole town entered vigorously into a state the anthropologist Victor Turner calls "liminality." Normal rules and social identities temporarily melted. Church deacons magically reappeared as dealers and *croupiers* at the blackjack table and the big-six wheel. Time and again local preachers tried to stop this open defiance of law and propriety, but they never succeeded. Peoples' needs for the festive will inevitably assert itself, no matter what. The primal energies will not be repressed indefinitely.

The dark underside of my town also sometimes came out. At Halloween the biggest parade of the year took place. It was originally instituted by the town fathers to provide something constructive for the kids to do and thereby to cut down on the number of garbage cans turned over and windows soaped. For weeks in advance, preparation for the parade kept everyone occupied. Sunday school classes, Legion posts, Girl Scout troops all designed and assembled thematic floats like *God Bless America* or *The Spirit of Temperance* or *Ghosts and Goblins*. A committee of distinguished town elders judged the entries as they passed by the reviewing stand, and handed out prizes. The freshly polished scarlet engines of the volunteer fire company always took part, noisily creeping past in their lowest gears. The Halloween parade was a splendid example of how civic virtue tries to keep the lid on the bawdier shades that are abroad that night.

But the spirit of misrule cannot be easily contained. While the handful of town police were directing traffic around the parade, the youthful marauders who did not belong to scout troops or Sunday school classes had a heyday with the unguarded garbage cans and windows. There were always more drunks in the streets. The atmosphere seemed lax, almost licentious. The attempt of political and religious elites to impose hegemony over unruly popular culture never works completely. Liminality will find a way. Our thirst for magic, for goblins, and for God is unquenchable.

The rebirth of festivity in our time is a sign of hope when we desperately need it, both politically and spiritually. Therefore, "*Que la fête commence!*" Let the Revels begin!

Feast of Fools

Harvey Cox

Revels makes a special place for the celebration known as the Feast of Fools. Back in 1969, just as Revels was beginning and long before I'd ever heard of it, I wrote a book about our culture's urgent need for a revival of the collective spirit embodied by the Feast of Fools.

DURING THE MEDIÆVAL ERA, there flourished in parts of Europe a holiday known as the Feast of Fools. On that colorful occasion, usually celebrated around January 1st, even ordinarily pious priests and serious townsfolk donned bawdy masks, sang outrageous ditties, and generally kept the whole world awake with revelry and satire. Minor clerics painted their faces, strutted about in the robes of their superiors, and mocked the stately rituals of church and court. Sometimes a Lord of Misrule, a Mock King, or a Boy Bishop was elected to preside over the event. During the Feast of Fools, no custom or convention was immune to ridicule and even the highest personages of the realm could expect to be lampooned.

The Feast of Fools was never popular with the higher-ups. It was constantly condemned and criticized. But, despite the efforts of fidgety ecclesiastics and an outright condemnation by the Council of Basel in 1431, the Feast of Fools survived until the 16th century. Then in the age of Reformation and Counter-Reformation it gradually died out. Its faint shade still persists in the pranks and revelry of Halloween and New Year's Eve.

Chroniclers of Western history seldom lament the passing of the Feast of Fools. Still, its death was a loss. It had demonstrated that a culture could periodically make sport of its most sacred royal and religious practices. It could imagine a wholly different kind of world - one where the last was first, accepted values were inverted, fools became kings, and choirboys were prelates. The demise of the Feast of Fools signaled a significant change in the Western cultural mood: an enfeeblement of our civilization's capacity for festivity and fantasy. Its demise showed that people were beginning to see their social roles and sacred conventions through eyes that could not permit such student satire, that they no longer had the time or the heart for such trenchant social parody.

Why did the Feast of Fools disappear? Why did the virtues of sobriety, thrift, industry and ambition gain such prominence at the expense of other values? Why did mirth, play and festivity come in for such scathing criticism during the Protestant era?

Festivity and fantasy do play a less central role among us now than they did in the days of holy fools, mystical visionaries and a calendar full of festivals. And we are the poorer for it.

There are those who would claim that we still have festivity and fantasy, but that they take a different form. We celebrate at office parties, football games and cocktail gatherings. Our fantasies glitter in the celluloid world of the cinema and on the pages of *Playboy*. Science fiction still conjures up fanciful worlds. Perhaps.

But my contention is that whatever forms of festivity and fantasy remain to us are shrunken and insulated. Our celebrations do not relate us, as they once did, to the parade of cosmic history or to the great stories of man's spiritual quest. Our fantasies tend to be cautious, eccentric, and secretive. When they do occasionally soar, they are appreciated only by an elite. Our feasting is sporadic or obsessive, our fantasies predictable and politically impotent. Neither provides the inspiration for genuine social transformation.

At least all of this has been true until quite recently. Now, however, we are witnessing a rebirth of the spirit of festivity and fantasy. Though we have no annual Feast of Fools, the life affirmation and playful irreverence once incarnated in that day are bubbling up again in our time. As expected, the bishops and the bosses are not happy about it, but it is happening anyway.

This incipient renaissance of fantasy and festivity is a good sign. It shows that our period may be rediscovering the value of two components of culture, both of which were once seen in the Feast of Fools. The first is the feast or festival itself: important because it puts work in its place. It suggests that work, however rewarding, is not the highest end of life but must contribute to personal human fulfillment. We need stated times for nonwork to remind us that not even an astronomical gross national product and total employment can bring a people salvation. On feast days we stop working and enjoy those traditional gestures and moments of human conviviality without which life would not be human.

Festivity, like play, contemplation, and making love, is an end in itself. It is not instrumental.

The other important cultural component of the Feast of Fools is fantasy and social criticism. Unmasking the pretense of the powerful always makes their power seem less irresistible. That is why tyrants tremble before fools and dictators ban political cabarets.

The Feast of Fools thus had an implicitly radical dimension. It exposed the arbitrary quality of social rank and enabled people to see that things need not always be as they are. Maybe that is why it made the power-wielders uncomfortable and eventually had to go. The divine right of kings, papal infallibility, and the modern totalitarian state all flowered after the Feast of Fools disappeared.

Today in the late twentieth-century we need the spirit represented by the Feast of Fools. In a success- and money-oriented society, we need a rebirth of patently unproductive festivity and expressive celebration. In an age that has quarantined parody and separated politics from imagination we need more social fantasy. We need for our time and in our own cultural idiom a rediscovery of what was right and good about the Feast of Fools. We need a renaissance of the spirit, and there are signs that it is coming.

◆

Revels is one of the forms in which that renaissance is manifesting.

The Fool as Healer

Elizabeth Lloyd Mayer

*O*NE OF THE GREAT healing figures in every culture is the figure of the Fool. Whether he appears as shaman, jester, trickster or clown, the Fool's wisdom is to see beyond human limitation – limitations of the body as well as of the mind and spirit. The Fool defies convention and in that defiance lie both his medicine and his magic. The Fool redefines what is possible.

In folk plays from all over the world, Fool figures have power over life and death; they bring healing when nothing else can. In the English mumming tradition, the Doctor never succeeds in reviving the slain hero, despite all his science and all his study. That is Fool's work. While he's making the audience laugh, the Fool foretells the magic that his foolery brings:

> *St. George shall come and die by swords*
> *which circle round his neck.*
> *As winter dies, so shall he die,*
> *and rise as spring again!*

In twentieth-century America, we lack a culture of the Fool. We work hard at everything and we take life seriously, whether we're focused on making money or leisure activity or keeping our bodies and souls in top condition. We have few rituals that remind us to laugh at ourselves and recognize how little we know, how little we really are able to control.

Theologian Harvey Cox describes how the medieval festival known as the Feast of Fools flourished throughout Europe.

It served to remind people that laughter and nonsense mattered. Hilarity, irreverence, and audacity were the order of the day as choirboys turned into prelates, servants became lords, and fools reigned as kings. Cox mourns the passing of the Feast of Fools in western culture. He sees a renewal of its spirit as key to healing our alienation from ourselves and from each other.

These days we also hear voices like Norman Cousins, Bernie Siegel and Joan Borysenko, along with those emerging from the new science of psycho-neuroimmunology. They remind us that laughter and lightness of spirit benefit our bodies. They tell us to defy prognoses, challenge preconceptions, be exceptions, expect the extraordinary. Like Cox, they are prescribing the wisdom of the Fool.

Cox suggests that, little by little, the Fool may be finding his (or, quite possibly, her) way back into our culture. Perhaps the Revels is one place this is happening. Through every Revels production, the figure of the Fool runs like a connecting thread. Every Christmas, Revels audiences watch that brief but extraordinary moment when the Fool turns nature back on itself, breathing life into the dead hero and turning winter back to spring. Actor Geoff Hoyle, veteran interpreter of the Fool, suggests that the astonishing variety and wild unpredictability of the Fool have one simple purpose: *"The Fool strips away our preconceptions so we can see the world as it might be."*

Increasingly, twentieth-century medicine teaches us that this stripping away – this learning to see ourselves as we might be – functions as the essence of healing. Perhaps the experience of seeing ourselves and the world as they might be, describes the essence of where Revels hopes to take us.

Hand in Hand

Peter Smith

I HAD NEVER HEARD of the Christmas Revels when I was approached by those hardy pioneers who wanted to bring them to Hanover, under the wing of the Hopkins Center. Of that much I am certain, but just about everything else concerning the early years of the Hanover Revels has been blocked out in my memory – perhaps from a desire on the part of an ex-administrator to forget as much as possible about the working life he has left behind, so that its miseries won't spoil the present as they spoiled the past and its pleasures won't tempt him back. But there is one thing I recall very clearly from the first time I attended a Revels performance: how disconcerted I was by the *"Lord of the Dance"* ritual, and how glad I was that, being in charge, I could avoid getting involved simply by getting up and going to the exit, without drawing too much attention to myself. In subsequent years, when being disconcerted was at its most painful, my response to the prospect of being drawn into the dancing chain was to head for the safety of the Spaulding Auditorium projection booth, from which I could watch and enjoy the music and take pleasure in the conviviality below me, without getting personally involved.

That kind of response continued for several years. It was not, of course, an isolated and unique thing in my life: I had always been one of those people in an audience who will not (cannot?) "join in the chorus" or clap their hands in time to the music when asked to do so. Thinking about, or especially writing about, the source of this particular inhibition would be quite beside the point; I simply need to establish the fact that I was very, very unwilling to be drawn in. And you need to know the strength of my reluctance in order to appreciate what it means to me that my reluctance has not merely disappeared, but has in fact been replaced by an eagerness to be a part of a ritual which has now become one of the annual blessings in my life.

That the Christmas Revels had a role in seeing that I have "turned out right" (to use the Shakers' own words for that magically simple melody) is something which will place me in its debt forever. It was only one part of a rather complex reworking of a rather complex life, a process in which I also changed my occupation to something more creative, recognized a talent or two that had been dormant for many years, and in general learned to open myself up to new possibilities in a way which my friends tell me has had a distinctly beneficial effect on my personality.

Offering this testimony to the power for good that can come if you reach out (reach out and touch someone[??!]) isn't meant to suggest that I have made a pilgrimage to Esalen and recommend that you do too; still less is it meant to put pressure on those who prefer to sit on their hands and get tickets as far from the aisles as possible so as to minimize the possibility of being seized by some enthusiast and dragged into the throng against their will. (Why, after all, should we *all* do the same thing at *any* time?) It is meant, rather, to pay tribute to the life-enhancing force of one small part of the Revels celebration and to say to anyone who may be hesitating, "I'm glad I took the plunge."

For me, the moment of taking to the aisles has become something very close to communion: I stay put (without, I hope, being ungracious to anyone who may thrust their hand in my direction) until I spot someone in the chain whom I know and admire or love, but do not see every day, and then I invite myself, as it were, into his or her hand. And once I'm on my feet I try to choose with care the people whom I reach out to – someone I wish I knew better, someone I know is at a low ebb, someone who seems to be on the brink of taking the plunge but can't quite do it. There are lots of good reasons for extending one's hand to a particular other hand.

I guess that underneath all my thoughts about this mini-transformation in my outlook are truths which inhabit George Herbert's moving poem *"Love bade me welcome, yet my soul drew back."* And that thought, following on others that have come to me as I have tried to set down my impressions of a significant personal experience connecting me to the Christmas Revels, has led to a realization that takes me by surprise. I have no idea – any more than anyone else has, of course – of what happens at the moment of death. But if it is something other than encountering oblivion, I realize that I cannot conceive of anything I would more joyfully welcome than having my hand taken by someone – a complete stranger, perhaps from the other side of the globe – who had died in the millisecond before me, someone who brings me into a very wide aisle and an infinitely long chain of people who are reveling in a dance which is a dance of life rather than a dance of death, people who are all connected, through their handholding, not only to one another but also, at the point where the line begins, to the one who is indeed the Lord of the Dance.

Contributors

THE REVEREND GEORGE BLACKMAN, a longtime student of history, was for thirty years rector of The Church of Our Saviour in Brookline, MA.

JOHN BREMER has been an eminent dancer and teacher for the English Folk Dance and Song Society and the Country Dance and Song Society. He has written on English dance and folklore, as well as on Plato and C.S. Lewis.

SUSAN COOPER is an author and screenwriter whose work includes the Newbery Award-winning sequence, *The Dark is Rising*. "A Dream of Revels" is a revised version of an article written for *The Horn Book Magazine* in 1979.

HARVEY COX is a Professor of Divinity at Harvard University and has written numerous books of social and theological commentary.

KATHERINE FIVEASH is a teacher, writer and environmentalist.

HUGH M. FLICK, JR. is a Sanskrit scholar and Dean of Silliman College at Yale University, where he teaches in Religious Studies. He wrote this essay on Revels while teaching Folklore and Mythology at Harvard University.

DOUGLAS KENNEDY, O.B.E., catalytic leader, choreographer, lecturer, dancer, author and teacher, succeeded Cecil Sharp as Director of the English Folk Dance and Song Society.

JOHN LANGSTAFF, concert artist and author of twenty-six children's books and song collections, is founder and Director Emeritus of Revels, Inc.

John H. Lienhard is the M.D. Anderson Professor in Mechanical Engineering and in History at the University of Houston. He writes and hosts "The Engines of Our Ingenuity," carried on numerous Public Radio stations nationally.

Gregory Maguire is the author of *Wicked: the Life and Times of the Wicked Witch of the West* and *Confessions of an Ugly Stepsister*, as well as a dozen books for children.

Elizabeth Lloyd Mayer is the founder and Artistic Director of California Revels and a Clinical Professor of Psychology at the University of California at Berkeley and the University of California Medical Center at San Francisco.

Peter Smith worked in the arts for institutions of higher education for forty years. In his second career, he is a professional actor and writer.

Patrick Swanson is the Artistic Director of Revels, Inc. He was raised in the North of England, where a few mummers and guisers still perform.

◆

"Feast of Fools" is reprinted with permission from Harvey Cox: *The Feast of Fools*. Cambridge, MA: Harvard University Press, 1969.

Kazuaki Tanahashi is a painter, writer, translator, and peace and environmental worker. Born in 1933 and trained as an artist in Japan, he has been based in the United States since 1977. Tanahashi has had many solo exhibitions of brushwork and presented many public painting performances in art galleries, universities, and museums around the world. He has written, translated, and edited over two dozen books, including *Brush Mind; Penetrating Laughter: Hakuin's Zen and Art; Moon in a Dewdrop: Writings of Zen Master Dogen;* and *Enlightenment Unfolds: The Essential Teachings of Zen Master Dogen.*

ABOUT REVELS was designed in the autumn of 2000 by George Mattingly and Elizabeth Lloyd Mayer. It was set at Studio GMD, Berkeley, in Eric Gill's Joanna roman and *Joanna* italic fonts, Timothy Donaldson's *John Handy* and Nicholas Cochin's **Cochin bold** and ***bold italic***.